Man Measures Man
A Play By
David Robson

For Sonja

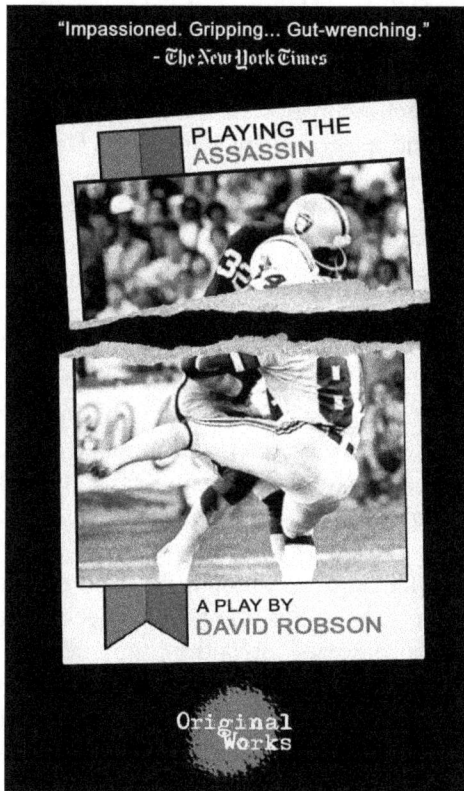

"Impassioned. Gripping... Gut-wrenching."
- The New York Times

PLAYING THE ASSASSIN

A PLAY BY
DAVID ROBSON

Original Works

PLAYING THE ASSASSIN

Synopsis: In a compelling drama about a man's legacy, former pro football player Frank Baker is offered the chance of a lifetime – an interview on CBS before the Super Bowl. But just when he thinks his luck has changed, Baker and his interviewer are blindsided by secrets and revelations. Inspired by a true story, this new play looks closely at hero worship and forgiveness. How will you be remembered when the final whistle is blown?

Cast Size: 2 Males

Man Measures Man premiered at the InterAct Theatre Company in Philadelphia, PA on March 2, 2001. The production was directed by Tim Moyer. The cast was comprised of Ralph Edmonds, Carol Florence, John Lumia, Laurie Norton, Matt Sanders and Ben White.

Characters:

THOMAS MANDELBAUM
Physician in his thirties

BEN GOLD
Physician in his thirties

TONYA RITTER
Nurse in her thirties or forties

AGIM ARIFI
Albanian in his mid-to-late teens
(Pronounced Ah-game.)

YULI
Serb in his forties

LUMINA ARIFI
Albanian in her forties or fifties

Time and Place:

April 1999. Macedonia, near the Kosovo border.

"War educates the senses, calls into action the will, and brings men into such swift and close collision that man measures man."
-Ralph Waldo Emerson

MAN MEASURES MAN

ACT I

SCENE 1

(In dark, sounds of vomiting. Light rises on THOMAS holding a disposable camera. BEN—doubled over and retching—is behind him. Duffel bags and suitcases are strewn about.)

THOMAS: I told you to get the chicken. Nobody gets the salmon on an airplane.

(He snaps a photo.)

BEN: Where the fuck are they?

THOMAS: Anybody's guess.

BEN: Great.

THOMAS: Relax.

BEN: Don't tell me to relax. We're in the middle of fucking nowhere and we probably missed our ride.

THOMAS: Whose fault is that, hotshot? *(He snaps another.)*

BEN: You're such a dick.

THOMAS: Look, we didn't miss our—

BEN: How do you know?

THOMAS: Because shit happens. Things get fucked up sometimes.

BEN: That's a relief.

THOMAS: You'll get used to it.

BEN: But they'd be crazy to forget about two MD's, right? They need us.

THOMAS: Absolutely.

BEN: We're on somebody's list.

THOMAS: Have to be. They're just a little slow getting here.

BEN: So this has happened before.

THOMAS: Happens all the time. You try and stay on a strict time schedule, but you know how things go. Maybe you don't. Anyway, there was this one time in Kigali, for instance. The driver shows up drunk off his ass—in no condition to drive. I mean, this guy was hammered—smelled like a Hong Kong whorehouse. Now, there's four of us—right? We'd just arrived. None of us speak the same language and we have no clue how the hell we're going to find the camp.

BEN: You think we're safe here?

THOMAS: Would you listen? So, we take the driver—he's passed out by now—and we roll him into the back seat of the car. I figure somebody's got to take charge of the situation, so I dig out this map that's in Swahili or something, and we all take off down this—

BEN: *(Seeing something.)* Oh shit!

THOMAS: What?

BEN: Isn't that—?

THOMAS: Where?

BEN: Over there? Right near the tree. Is that them? I...

THOMAS: What was it?

BEN: Thought I saw some movement by the tree.

THOMAS: Just keep your eyes open.

(THOMAS digs into his bag and pulls out a few items before finding his cell phone. He begins to dial.)

BEN: You love this, don't you?

THOMAS: What's that?

BEN: Getting stranded like this.

THOMAS: Are you crazy?

BEN: Look at you: you've got the cell phone, the map. You're a regular Goddamned Boy Scout.

THOMAS: *(Frustrated with phone.)* Shit.

BEN: This is what you went into medicine to do, huh, come to places like this?

THOMAS: Beats the hell out of living the Main Line doctor scene. Can you imagine my dad out here?

BEN: There's nothing wrong with wanting a normal practice.

THOMAS: You'd know I guess.

BEN: What's that supposed to mean?

THOMAS: Hey, I do good work, get to travel...I'm telling you, thousands of these people come and go right in front of you. You never even get to know their names. But you get their blood on your shirt, and you send them back better than you found them.

BEN: I guess it beats skydiving.

THOMAS: Want to go home already?

BEN: No, I—

THOMAS: We just got here.

BEN: I'm just—

THOMAS: I tried to warn you.

BEN: Uh huh.

THOMAS: Then again, letters are a dying art.

BEN: At least the way *you* write them.

THOMAS: Maybe I should have thrown in a few pictures.

BEN: You might have scared me off.

THOMAS: You could have said no, like all the other times.

BEN: Not this time.

THOMAS: What made the difference?

BEN: Oh, I don't know…couple of beers, a few laughs…

THOMAS: Promise of an all expense paid trip to Eastern Europe.

BEN: You said Prague.

THOMAS: I lied.

BEN: I noticed.

THOMAS: Seriously.

BEN: Seriously? What was I staying home for?

THOMAS: You tell me.

BEN: I just did.

(Beat.)

THOMAS: You know, Ben…

BEN: What's that?

THOMAS: I know I never…

BEN: What?

THOMAS: I wanted to be there, you know. I really—I tried to get away…

BEN: Sure you did.

THOMAS: I did.

BEN: I believe you.

THOMAS: You wouldn't believe how hard it is to book a flight from—

BEN: Look—

THOMAS: Even the charters aren't—

BEN: You don't have to explain.

THOMAS: I know I don't.

BEN: Then don't, alright? *(Beat.)* Hey, did you notice the looks we were getting at the airport?

THOMAS: From who—the security guys? Who cares?

BEN: It's just kind of ironic: we're here, but nobody *here* likes us. Eastern Europe isn't exactly the Promised Land, if you—

THOMAS: Don't get started—

BEN: Does that look like a van over there?

THOMAS: Where?

BEN: *(Pointing.)* Over there! Didn't you—?

THOMAS: What?

BEN: It's gone.

THOMAS: Think it was our guy?

BEN: You're the expert.

THOMAS: I never said that.

BEN: It's getting dark.

THOMAS: I can see.

BEN: So what's taking so long? I thought you knew the guy who runs the camp.

THOMAS: I do.

BEN: Some Swede.

THOMAS: Andersson, yeah. So what?

BEN: You'd think that if you guys were such great pals—Hey, there he is again. See him?

THOMAS: Grab your shit.

BEN: Wait a minute. Flag him down.

THOMAS: Put your hand down!

BEN: But it might be our ride.

THOMAS: *(Gathering bags.)* Does it look like our ride?

BEN: How am I supposed to know?

THOMAS: Use your head. We're walking.

BEN: There's no way I'm—

THOMAS: I said grab your shit. We're not in Kansas anymore, Ben. Move!

(They exit quickly as lights fade.)

(A small tent city. TONYA, her back turned, is talking on her cell phone. The connection is bad.)

TONYA: …But I'm not interested in another—There's been too much media attention already. What's that? You're breaking—I said I'm losing you. Huh? Well, what I'm saying is—Yes, there is such a thing as—Uh huh, when it infringes upon the lives of—I can't hear you—

(THOMAS enters with bags; BEN trails him, wiped out.)

THOMAS: *(Yelling as he enters.)* What are you doing to us, old man?

TONYA: *(To THOMAS and BEN)* Hey, can keep it—?

THOMAS: Huh?

TONYA: Keep it—! *(Into phone.)* Not you. *(To THOMAS and BEN.)* You can't put your bags there?

THOMAS: Yeah, yeah, sure.

TONYA: *(Into phone.)* I wasn't talking—

THOMAS: What the hell happened to—?

TONYA: *(To THOMAS)* Would you just—*(Into phone.)* Uh huh. Yeah.

THOMAS: Where's Gus Andersson?

TONYA: *(TO THOMAS and BEN)* You'll have to wait!

THOMAS: We've been waiting long enough!

TONYA: *(Into phone)* I'm going to have to call you back. Hello…? Hello…?

(TONYA loses the connection.)

BEN: We're the new docs.

THOMAS: Now, where's that sack of shit Swede hiding out?

TONYA: Dr. Andersson is in Chechnya.

BEN: What?

TONYA: He won't be running this operation.

THOMAS: You're kidding.

TONYA: I'm the hospital coordinator.

THOMAS: Nobody told me about this.

TONYA: Is there a problem?

THOMAS: Yeah, we waited for over an hour at the way-point.

TONYA: Somebody must have dropped the ball.

THOMAS: Damn right they did!

BEN: Had to walk the rest of the way.

TONYA: *(Extending hand.)* You must be Dr. Gold. I'm Tonya Ritter.

17

BEN: Ben. How did you know?

TONYA: Last arrivals of the day. And Doctor Mandelbaum and I have met before.

THOMAS: Have we?

TONYA: You don't remember.

THOMAS: Uh...

BEN: *(Under his breath.)* There's a surprise.

TONYA: Five years ago. Haiti.

THOMAS: Haiti. Sure. You worked...um...

TONYA: Obstetrics.

THOMAS: Obstetr—*(He remembers.)* Right.

TONYA: Right.

THOMAS: Hey, uh, sorry about the, uh...I just assumed Andersson was running the show. See, we have this little thing going: He busts my balls and I—

TONYA: I gathered.

THOMAS: Right. *(Beat.)* So, what have you been up to? Been on any operations since Haiti?

TONYA: No. You?

THOMAS: Me? Oh yeah. Been to Rwanda, Algeria, Laos... uh... Bosnia a couple of times, Afghanistan... What have you been doing with yourself?

TONYA: After Haiti, I went home for a while to finish my master's.

BEN: On top of your M.D.?

TONYA: No.

BEN: No?

TONYA: No M.D. R.N.

BEN: Oh.

TONYA: You can pick up your medical kits and other supplies in tent 5.

THOMAS: Sounds good.

TONYA: As usual, we're running 12 hour shifts. You start immediately.

BEN: Immediately?

TONYA: You're four hours late.

THOMAS: Ben got a little sick on the way. He might need a few—

BEN: I was hoping we could take a few minutes.

THOMAS: You can give us half an hour to clean up, can't you Tonya?

TONYA: I wish I could...

THOMAS: I'd really appreciate it.

TONYA: But we've already got long lines with your names on them. We have 4500 Albanians crossing the every—

THOMAS: I'll need to wash up before surgery.

TONYA: Not possible.

THOMAS: What do you mean, not possible?

(TONYA's cell phone rings.)

TONYA: No water. *(Answering the phone.)* Ritter. *(Listens briefly.)* Yup, I'm on it. Hold on. *(To THOMAS.)* We're waiting for a fresh shipment. But we have plenty of surgical gloves.

BEN: You have *got* to be kidding. You can't expect us to work like this.

TONYA: Welcome to Macedonia, Dr. Gold. *(As lights fade, back on the phone.)* Hey, what's the ETA on the water? *(Listens.)* Uh huh. Well, we don't have that kind of time. Tell him—look, I don't care if his dog had kittens—I need it yesterday, alright…?

SCENE 3

(BEN and THOMAS— shifts done—meet on the way to their tent. They both wear medical scrubs, and THOMAS carries a bottle of clear liquor.)

THOMAS: Don't you play a doctor on TV?

BEN: I wish I did. The money's got to be better. What's in the bottle?

THOMAS: Rakija **(Rah-ki).** Local firewater. Thought we might celebrate.

BEN: What's the occasion?

THOMAS: You survived your first week.

BEN: Are you sure I survived it?

THOMAS: You're still standing, aren't you? I've seen docs fall apart after two hours in a place like this. The volume fucks them up.

BEN: I just hide it well.

THOMAS: Count your blessings, pal. They send me the bomb victims.

BEN: Yeah, well, they send me the kids.

THOMAS: Ah well, look at it this way, if NATO keeps dropping bombs we'll have the market cornered: we maim them, we mend them, right?

BEN: Makes me realize how easy I had it.

THOMAS: You're not kidding.

(They arrive at their tent. Apart from the cots, it contains a small table, which has a chessboard and pieces. On BEN'S cot is a letter, half-written.)

BEN: I don't want to think about it anymore. Sleep. Sleep...

THOMAS: The night is young. You can't crash on me now.

BEN: We're up again in, like, two hours.

THOMAS: That's what I mean. What's the point of sleeping?

BEN: *(Rolling over in his cot.)* I just need some shut-eye before they bring in the next round.

THOMAS: *(Spotting letter.)* Looks like you have a lot to say.

BEN: Will you leave my shit alone, please?

THOMAS: "Dear Jess?" You have got to be kidding me!

BEN: Leave it—!

THOMAS: I'm not letting you do this.

BEN: Give it to me.

THOMAS: I have a duty to take this kind of thing—

BEN: Since when?

THOMAS: Since always.

BEN: Oh yeah? So where you been the last—?

THOMAS: I always returned your calls.

BEN: Yeah, three weeks later.

THOMAS: Come on, Ben. Give me one good reason to write to her.

BEN: I thought she'd like to know.

THOMAS: About what?

BEN: About this—what's going on here.

THOMAS: Oh brother. Do you know how this makes you sound?

BEN: It's not a big deal.

THOMAS: Glad to hear it.

(THOMAS crumples letter.)

BEN: Don't!

THOMAS: It's for your own good.

BEN: I'll just write another one when you're not around.

(THOMAS reluctantly hands BEN the letter.)

THOMAS: She'll never write you back, you know.

BEN: It doesn't matter.

THOMAS: Then why send it if it doesn't matter? How long has it been—two, three months?

BEN: Five next—

THOMAS: Five! Separated for almost a year; divorce papers go through five months ago—

BEN: Can we just drop it?

THOMAS: ...And here you sit, thousands of miles from home—

BEN: We were married for 8 years.

THOMAS: Eight years too long if you ask—

BEN: Yeah, well, she never liked you much either.

THOMAS: You've just got to let it go, Benji. It's over.

BEN: I realize...

THOMAS: Like hell you do.

BEN: Oh yeah? And what would you know about it? Why don't you tell me about your longest relationship there, Big T?

THOMAS: *(Pouring the rakija and passing it to BEN for a toast.)* All I'm saying, Ben, is that we're here now, just the two of us. Like old times. *(They drink.)* And if you need somebody to talk to—

BEN: I'll be fine.

(Silence. BEN tries to sleep.)

THOMAS: Your move.

BEN: I'm tired!

THOMAS: Come on. You remember how we used to pull a forty-eight hour shift and then play for six hours straight?

BEN: It was never six. Three maybe.

THOMAS: Whatever. Come on, just a taste.

(BEN rises and moves his pawn forward.)

BEN: Happy?

THOMAS: Now we're in business. Let me see…hmm…

(Long pause.)

BEN: Can we move this along, please?

THOMAS: I'm thinking, alright?

BEN: What's there to think about? We just started.

THOMAS: *(Moving.)* By the way, you met Dr. Radulovic?

BEN: Radulovic?

THOMAS: One of the recovery team docs. They patrol the border and pick up the more seriously injured refugees—the ones who can't make it to camp. Radulovic heads it up.

BEN: *(Surveying board and moving.)* Oh yeah, what's he like?

THOMAS: It's a she.

BEN: Ah, that's why I haven't seen much of you lately.

THOMAS: Maja Radulovic.

BEN: Like the name. Where's she from?

THOMAS: Montenegro. Two countries over.

BEN: Let me guess: Dark hair; pouty lips; *(Imitating)* *thick* Balkan accent.

THOMAS: You've met.

BEN: Let's just say that some things never change.

THOMAS: Least of all me.

BEN: Most of all you.

THOMAS: What can I say?

BEN: Sounds like she's just your speed.

THOMAS: We're cruising in low gear to start.

BEN: Now that's not like you at all.

THOMAS: She even talked me into riding to the border with the team one day, check it out. They're seeing some serious shit.

BEN: Could be dangerous.

THOMAS: Guess it beats skydiving.

BEN: Uh huh.

THOMAS: I'll probably have to switch shifts with somebody.

BEN: Don't look at me.

THOMAS: Thanks pal. Actually, I was thinking of hitting up one of the Israeli docs.

BEN: Worth a shot.

THOMAS: Although, have you noticed…?

BEN: What?

THOMAS: They're kind of…you know…

BEN: They've been fine to me.

THOMAS: Hey, they've got three of them working OR and you should see the attitudes.

BEN: It does kind of come with the territory, doesn't it?

THOMAS: Come on, Ben, this isn't fucking Gaza.

BEN: You're unbelievable. You'd think places like this would put you a little more in touch with where you came from.

THOMAS: I came from Philly, just like you.

BEN: You know what I mean, shit head.

THOMAS: Settle down. I thought you were tired.

BEN: I am. I was. *(Reaching for rakija.)* What's that stuff called?

THOMAS: *(Moving it.)* I think you've had enough, Benji. You're becoming belligerent.

BEN: You started it.

THOMAS: Besides, I'm saving the rest for a *special* occasion.

BEN: Oh really?

THOMAS: Never know when it might come in handy with the ladies—

(A loud thump is heard.)

THOMAS (Cont'd): What the hell is that?

BEN: Sounds like Dr. Radulovic's right on time.

(AGIM appears from the shadows, his neck bloody. THOMAS stands, knocking over chessboard. AGIM collapses.)

BEN (Cont'd): Holy shit!

(They rush to the boy's aid as lights fade.)

SCENE 4

(BEN, stethoscope around his neck, is rereading the crumpled letter from Scene 3, crossing out some of what is written, and rewriting.)

BEN: *(Under his breath.)* "Dear Jess"…Shit…

*(AGIM enters. He carries **The Happy Isles of Oceania** by Paul Theroux. BEN notices him, folds his letter, and puts it away.)*

BEN (Cont'd): Good morning, come on in. I'm Dr. Gold. *(He takes something from his pocket.)* I understand you've been looking for this. (It's a *black Chicago Bulls knit hat*.)

AGIM: Yes.

(BEN tosses AGIM the hat. AGIM opens it, peers inside, and then puts it on.)

BEN: Be careful of your bandage there.

AGIM: Yes.

BEN: How's the book? Have a seat.

AGIM: I like fiction better, but this is all they have today.

BEN: His stuff is pretty good actually.

AGIM: What else did he write?

BEN: Oh, some novels, but I like the travel books best.

AGIM: I would like to see Australia.

BEN: How does he make it sound?

AGIM: Backward. Small minded.

BEN: And you'd like to go there?

AGIM: Sound like home.

(Beat.)

BEN: How you feeling?

AGIM: O-kay.

BEN: You scared us the other night.

AGIM: I do not mean. I look for place to pee. I get lost.

BEN: There's a bottle next to your bed so you don't have
    to go anywhere.

AGIM: I cannot pee with others around.

BEN: The modest type, huh? *(Beat.)* So, you're here for a
    follow-up.

AGIM: Yes.

BEN: *(Checking chart.)* I see you're leaving us tomorrow.

AGIM: That is what *she* say.

BEN: She who?

AGIM: Ritter.

BEN: Ah.

AGIM: I tell her I need to stay, but she does not listen. She does not care for what happens to me.

BEN: *(Checking AGIM'S vision and pulse.)* She does, but she has a lot of responsibilities. You're not our only patient.

AGIM: I do not like her.

BEN: Give her a break.

AGIM: American nurses supposed to be sweet and sexy with sensitive bedside manner—and big tits.

BEN: You watch too much television.

AGIM: Enough to know.

BEN: Well, I'm sure she'll be sorry to know she disappointed you.

AGIM: You do not have to tell her these things.

BEN: I won't. Alright, take off your shirt.

(AGIM does. BEN begins checking his ribs.)

AGIM: Where you from?

BEN: Philadelphia.

AGIM: Liberty Bell.

BEN: You got it.

AGIM: How long you here?

BEN: About a week.

AGIM: You glad you come?

BEN: I'm still getting used to the idea, to be honest. *(He begins checking AGIM's neck.)*

AGIM: You have wife, family?

BEN: What's that?

AGIM: You have wife and family in Phila-del-phia?

BEN: No wife.

AGIM: Why you wear ring then?

BEN: I, uh, I *was* married.

AGIM: She die?

BEN: Alright, quit it with the questions.

AGIM: Answer.

BEN: We're divorced, actually.

AGIM: Why you still wear it?

BEN: Habit, I guess.

AGIM: Children?

BEN: No.

AGIM: Why?

BEN: Okay kid, get dressed.

AGIM: Why?

BEN: Because the exam is done. There's no reason we shouldn't let you go.

AGIM: I am still sick. I feel it.

BEN: I don't think so. You've felt better, sure, but vital signs are looking good, your neck wound is healing nicely. And since you haven't shut up since you got here, my diagnosis is—

AGIM: You know why I am talking now and not much before? When I first come in I do not talk to others much. I keep to myself. People ask me things, but I do not tell them. You want to know why?

BEN: Is it a secret?

AGIM: When you do not talk you can listen. Listening, you hear who to trust. You cannot trust everybody. I trust you.

BEN: You're sure you've got the right guy? Hospitals are crawling with guys that look just like me—almost like me. I'm a little better looking than most.

AGIM: No you not.

BEN: It was a joke.

AGIM: It was not funny.

BEN: I'll try harder next time.

AGIM: I watch when I first come. I was listening. Because when you not talking…

BEN: You're listening. It's a beautiful thing.

AGIM: What is?

BEN: Your strategy. Play sick until you can get an eye-ful—

AGIM: Earful. I was hurt.

BEN: Yes.

AGIM: I feel better now.

BEN: And that's why we're sending you out.

AGIM: I do not want to go. If I had money, I would pay.

BEN: What's there to stay for? Latrines are backed up; the water's slow in coming; and all the mess tent seems to serve is lentil soup.

AGIM: I like soup.

BEN: We're far too crowded to keep you.

AGIM: But I have to stay for mother.

BEN: What's your mother's name? Maybe she came in today.

AGIM: Her name is Lu...Lu...Lumina.

BEN: *(Checking.)* Lumina Arifi. No, I don't have her on my list, but this isn't the latest one. If we find her, I'll have someone let you know.

AGIM: Come right away. Fast.

BEN: Right away. Yes.

AGIM: I need to know she alright.

BEN: Of course you do. You only have one mother.

AGIM: Yes. And she is mine.

BEN: And what happens if you find your mother?

AGIM: I do not... know... I do not know... But if I am sent to camp in Skopje we lose one another. There will not be way to find her.

BEN: We're keeping excellent records. If she gets here she'll be given immediate medical attention. She'll be interviewed, and then her name will be matched with yours.

AGIM: If you try and send me away I play sick again.

BEN: I think you let the cat out of the bag on that one.

AGIM: Cat out...?

BEN: It's an expression—not important.

AGIM: I will hurt myself. You send me back, I am as good as dead. You must help me.

BEN: There's nothing more I can do. I appreciate the drama, but we only have so many supplies, so many beds.

AGIM: I give up my bed. I sleep in mud.

BEN: I can't let you do that.

AGIM: But you not like other doctors. I see that. I see when you fix woman's broken leg or pull old man's tooth. Other doctors rush around—they help but don't take time to talk, to touch. Many can't see what people here need—can't see what we been in—places where nobody cares and only want us to die. You listen—like me—you listen. That's why I *think* I can trust you.

BEN: You *can* trust me.

AGIM: It is a beautiful thing.

BEN: Look, A-jim—

AGIM: *(Correcting pronunciation.)* Agim.

BEN: Agim. I can promise you this: I'll get your exact whereabouts—Nurse Ritter can find this out. If your mother comes—

AGIM: When!

BEN: *When* your mother comes, I will personally assure her that you are safe and well. If you've listened and watched me enough, you know that I don't lie to people.

(YULI enters. He is seen only by AGIM.)

36

AGIM: What do you know?

YULI: I know more than you think, boy. These people have their own country. It wears their name, for Christ's sake.

AGIM: Do you like trains?

BEN: What?

AGIM: Trains. Do you like them?

YULI: What we are doing here is returning things to their natural order.

BEN: Sure. I like trains all right.

YULI: We do shit work, but we reap the rewards too.

AGIM: What do you like about them?

BEN: I've never thought about it really.

AGIM: Is it sound?

BEN: The sound? Maybe. I don't know.

YULI: As much as people say that we have to live together, we are not going to live somewhere we do not belong. They are not either.

AGIM: You like train whistle?

BEN: I guess I like the sound of the train coming to a halt.

YULI: You can see that by now. You are old enough.

AGIM: As I was making my way out—toward border, I passed Polje. Have you heard of it? Polje?

BEN: No, but I expect that Polje has a train station?

AGIM: Polje has our country's biggest train station.

YULI: Oh well, what do I know? I am just a bitter old man, long past his prime.

AGIM: I passed Polje everyday to go to school. I know conductors. Sometimes I get free ride. Or they blow whistle for me.

YULI: That is what you say to yourself, isn't it, boy?

AGIM: That is sound I loved. I was leaving last week; I had to pass Polje train station one more time. The Serbs had been there. I listened. No whistle. What is train station without sound of whistle?

YULI: But you mark my words...

AGIM: In station I saw bodies: Four Muslims—hunks of charred meat. One, covered with blood, face black from beating and fire, was propped against door—a warning.

YULI: You will see what they do to us if they ever get the chance.

AGIM: This is last Albanian I see before here.

YULI: And with fucking Americans involved forget it. They'll piss away twenty, thirty million and drop smart bombs on us.

AGIM: I do not forget these things. I write it all down. *(AGIM pulls a journal from his pants.)* It is here. In English mostly.

BEN: In English...

AGIM: At first I go back and forth—between English and... and... but now... It is practice. *(Pointing in journal.)* Here is new word: *dis-ori-ent.*

BEN: Very good.

AGIM: I get better. Grammar is hard.

YULI: I don't want to be carrying you out there. You are either ready to be a man or I'll leave you home sewing with the women.

BEN: You like to write.

AGIM: I like to read more.

YULI: Which is it?

AGIM: Back in Kosova that is all I do.

YULI: I saw you carrying something.

AGIM: I like Conrad, Kundera, Camus.

YULI: Books?

AGIM: A neighbor let me borrow them.

YULI: They are a waste of your time, boy.

AGIM: Do you have many?

BEN: I've got a house full.

YULI: These writers spout garbage from their minds, but they cannot reconcile the fact that it is people like us who make a difference in this world, not them. Nobody gives a shit what they think. We are the ones left to settle things—once and for all.

AGIM: Once it is over I go back.

BEN: I'll have to send you some once you've—you know—settled.

AGIM: But mother needs me. She is all family I have left. And I am only son, you see. Man of house. If you have son—Do you? If you did you would understand. Where I come from, Serbs want to kill all—

(THOMAS enters; YULI exits.)

THOMAS: What's going on?

BEN: Oh, hey.

THOMAS: Quite a line you got out there.

BEN: I'm…I'm almost done with Agim here.

THOMAS: *(Recognizing AGIM.)* You scared the shit out of us the other night.

BEN: This is Dr. Mandelbaum.

AGIM: Hello.

(THOMAS extends hand. They shake.)

THOMAS: Great hat.

AGIM: Thanks.

THOMAS: Get many games over here?

AGIM: Sometimes newspapers show scores.

THOMAS: Bulls haven't been the same since the big guy
    left, huh?

AGIM: Bulls suck without Jordan, yes.

(THOMAS and BEN laugh.)

THOMAS: *(To BEN.)* So what gives?

BEN: Agim is scheduled for discharge tomorrow. I just
    gave him a clean bill of health.

THOMAS: Glad to hear it.

AGIM: *(To THOMAS.)* You do E-MER-GES-CY.

THOMAS: You're good, kid. *(To BEN.)* He's good.

AGIM: I like to practice English big words.

BEN: Agim was just telling me about his favorite au-
    thors: Conrad, Kundera…Who was the other one?

AGIM: Camus.

BEN: How could I forget?

THOMAS: Didn't Camus write that thing about—what was it? Shit—the guy who spends eternity in hell pushing a huge boulder up a hill?

BEN/AGIM: Sisyphus.

THOMAS: Sisyphus, right. Problem is the damn thing keeps rolling back down.

BEN: Sounds familiar.

THOMAS: Story of my life. *(To AGIM.)* You can go now, guy. I need to speak with Dr. Gold.

(AGIM gathers his book and journal and exits.)

BEN: Sweet kid, huh?

THOMAS: What's the diagnosis?

BEN: Laceration to the neck, couple of broken ribs.

THOMAS: How big was the laceration?

BEN: Three centimeters. From a gunshot.

THOMAS: There's a surprise.

BEN: It's taking a while to heal.

THOMAS: They always do. And, by the way, if you get done this century, take a look at the board: You're in deep shit.

BEN: We'll see about that. *(THOMAS goes to leave.)* Hey Tom.

THOMAS: Hey Ben.

BEN: I, uh, finally met your friend Dr. Radulovic.

THOMAS: Oh yeah?

BEN: I didn't realize she went to med school in the States.

THOMAS: Harvard.

BEN: She might just teach you a thing or two.

THOMAS: I'm counting on it.

BEN: I was thinking…maybe I'll make a border run with you sometime. Check out the front lines.

THOMAS: You'd shit your pants.

BEN: You been out on one yet?

THOMAS: Not yet. I'm going to try to get Tonya to schedule me for next week.

BEN: So this is serious with Maja.

THOMAS: What serious?

BEN: What's wrong with that?

THOMAS: Nothing, but I wouldn't say—

BEN: Come on.

THOMAS: I'm having a blast talking to her—different culture, different perspective on things—that's all.

BEN: Better watch out. That's how it all gets started.

THOMAS: Not for me. Then again…

BEN: What?

THOMAS: Nothing. I think the lack of sleep is finally catching up with me.

BEN: Listen, I want to get your opinion on something.

THOMAS: *(Checking watch.)* Yeah, sure, make it fast, huh.

BEN: I'm trying to decide—I'm…I'm…thinking about maybe postponing Agim's discharge another day or two.

THOMAS: You said they're sending him out when?

BEN: Tomorrow. Been here six days or so.

THOMAS: You ask him how he stumbled into our tent?

BEN: He was *disoriented*—couldn't find his way back to bed. He's still a bit unstable. I'd like to keep an eye on that laceration.

THOMAS: Just use your discretion. You're the doc.

BEN: He's also waiting for his, uh, his mother.

THOMAS: They're all waiting for somebody, Ben. They can keep an eye on his injury in Skopje.

BEN: She might be right behind him. It might only be another day.

AGIM: *(Peaking back in.)* Doctor Gold?

THOMAS: Yeah, and it could be three weeks. Load him on the bus already.

AGIM: Doctor Gold!

BEN: Yes.

AGIM: Do you think I could go check refugee list?

BEN: That's fine. Just make sure to get some rest.

AGIM: I will.

(They watch as AGIM exits again.)

THOMAS: A little warm for the hat, isn't it?

BEN: Kind of. Funny to see them wearing our stuff.

THOMAS: Send them enough of our shit and we can wipe out any culture faster than a boatload of anthrax. *(Beat.)* So, what makes...what makes...?

BEN: Agim.

THOMAS: What makes Agim worth all the attention?

BEN: He's been ripped away from his home; he's intelligent; he's...

THOMAS: Ah, we're just treating the smart ones. Glad you told me, because I've got a ward full of total idiots.

BEN: That's not what I mean. Look, all I have to do is write in his chart—

THOMAS: So you're going to lie for this kid now?

BEN: You're telling me you've never tweaked a chart to help a patient out a little.

THOMAS: Sure, but I don't make a habit out of it.

BEN: What habit? This is one kid.

THOMAS: They just posted the latest bed count. Did you see that? We're down to three. If you're smart you'll just sign his release and send him on his way tomorrow, as scheduled.

(As lights fade on THOMAS and BEN, they rise on AGIM, wearing his hat down almost over his eyes. He is carrying a bowl of soup, which he slurps, and is eyeing an updated refugee list.)

SCENE 5

(BEN is entering; THOMAS is lying in his cot.)

THOMAS: Are you playing or not?

BEN: I'm playing.

THOMAS: Then move. I'm in surgery in half an hour.

BEN: *(Surveying board.)* Uh…

THOMAS: Come on, come on.

BEN: Don't rush me.

THOMAS: I'm growing a beard here.

BEN: Fine, uh, Knight takes bishop.

THOMAS: *(Looking.)* Where?

BEN: *(Pointing.)* Right…there!

THOMAS: You sure you want to do that? You don't want to look at the whole board?

BEN: I am.

THOMAS: Leave it then. Knight takes bishop.

(Pause.)

BEN: Maybe I'll take it back.

THOMAS: Okay. I'll allow it—this time.

BEN: Nah, nah, nah, I'm not going to beat your ass and then let you tell me I cheated.

THOMAS: First of all, there's no way you're beating my ass.

BEN: My, aren't we a little cocky today—?

THOMAS: And secondly, I expect you to cheat.

BEN: Good. My move stays then. Take your time.

THOMAS: Queen takes Queen. Checkmate.

BEN: Shit!

THOMAS: You fall for it every time, Benji. All you see is the one move, and that's suicide. You've got to look at the big—

TONYA: *(Calling from outside.)* Ben, are you in there?

(TONYA enters, arms full of paperwork, and plops it all down on their chess board.)

THOMAS: Watch out!

TONYA: *(To BEN.)* Finish these.

BEN: Right now?

TONYA: Your paperwork is piling up.

BEN: I just got off.

TONYA: A lot of the people you're seeing have minor injuries to begin with, but you're scheduling them for follow-ups.

BEN: Pretty normal, don't you think?

TONYA: Not here. We need the room. *(Checks one of the forms.)* Look at this one: a woman. Nadia Stankovic. 56. Came in dehydrated and complaining of stomach pains. You did two follow-ups before sending her to Skopje.

BEN: May I see that, please? It says here she was *severely* dehydrated. We pumped some fluid into her. I didn't think it made sense to send her out until she was stabilized and that took a few days.

TONYA: Five days. That's too long.

BEN: Says who?

TONYA: Says me. This isn't like your regular practice.

BEN: With all due respect, I think you're overstepping your medical—

TONYA: I did the numbers. The rest of the medical staff is seeing about 30% more patients than you are. We can't afford the extra time right now; there was a lot of NATO bombing last night. We're expecting a huge convoy of refugees and we'll probably get at least half of them tomorrow morning.

THOMAS: How many is that?

TONYA: 8-to-12,000.

BEN: 12,000!

THOMAS: For fuck's sake!

TONYA: Most of the people here will have to be moved out as soon as possible.

BEN: Alright, I get the picture. I'll try to speed these along.

TONYA: And what about Agim?

BEN: Agim?

TONYA: I scheduled him for discharge the other day, but he's still here.

THOMAS: Ben.

TONYA: Or, was that supposed to be a secret? Because if it was, you should have told Agim. I saw him twenty minutes ago over by the supply tent. He gave me the biggest wave.

BEN: I was planning to speak to you.

TONYA: Is that right? Because while it may not be clear to you, it is crystal clear to me that Agim's mother is either lost or dead—

BEN: You don't know—

TONYA: —And that keeping him here goes against every protocol of this camp, not to mention agency policy. If we bend the rules for Agim, then others will expect the same treatment.

THOMAS: Things don't work that way around here—

TONYA: You're defending this?

THOMAS: I'm not defending—

TONYA: I have a responsibility to keep an entire camp running, and every day Agim stays is another day we have to provide his food and water, and somebody else might have to go without. Now, the good news is Agim's one of the lucky ones. He has family in New Jersey.

THOMAS: I wouldn't call that lucky exactly.

TONYA: They've been contacted; an uncle on his mother's side has agreed to accept him. There's a bus leaving for Skopje tomorrow, and Agim needs to be on it. I'll expect the rest of these forms completed by 1400 hours. *(Turns to go but remembers something.)* By the way, Thomas, I talked to Maja Radulovic today. She tells me you've volunteered for recovery.

THOMAS: Thought I might be of service.

TONYA: I'll see about putting you on the schedule as soon as we manage this new wave of people. I must say, Dr. Radulovic seemed awfully anxious to get you on her team.

(TONYA exits.)

BEN: I'm not even *touching* that one.

THOMAS: What are you doing?

BEN: What do you mean?

THOMAS: You said you'd tell her, Ben.

BEN: I said I'd do the right thing.

THOMAS: The right thing for who?

BEN: For Agim.

THOMAS: For you.

BEN: This isn't about me. I'm looking at Agim's story and—

THOMAS: Our job is to fix as many people as possible.

BEN: Yes, and it starts with a single person. And if that means I get a little backed-up—

THOMAS: A little backed up? You heard what Tonya said: you're in the weeds. And she's not the only one saying it.

BEN: What are you talking about?

THOMAS: Let's just say you're getting a reputation. Look, I don't want to get into this right now.

BEN: You're already in it.

(Beat.)

THOMAS: Let's just say a few of the docs—

BEN: Like who?

THOMAS: I don't know—Reese, Hurley...

BEN: To hell with them.

THOMAS: Fine, to hell with them, but you're starting to make me look bad. I told these people what a top flight physician you are and—

BEN: Well fuck you, too.

THOMAS: Don't take it like that.

BEN: How am I supposed to take it? First you question my motives, and now you're telling me how to be a doctor?

THOMAS: I'm telling you how to be a doctor *here*, Ben. That's all. You're not used to this kind of environment.

BEN: Don't patronize me.

THOMAS: It's the truth! You're spending too much time with these—

BEN: Yeah, and maybe you're not spending enough.

THOMAS: Don't try to turn this around.

BEN: What happened to you?

THOMAS: When?

BEN: You've become so goddamned clinical. How can you be so cold and removed about what's happening here?

THOMAS: Hey, I'm not the one holding things up.

BEN: All I know is that your father is the kind of man—

THOMAS: Are you crazy? He never did what *we're* doing?

BEN: Just because the guy didn't sacrifice his career to treat Ebola victims at the South Pole doesn't make him any less of—

THOMAS: Who's sacrificing—?

BEN: You come here, where nobody can see your work.

THOMAS: That's not what this is about—

BEN: You do this hack surgery—

THOMAS: Hack surgery? Now—

BEN: And you walk around pretending that you're God's gift to medicine. But you know something, Thomas? You couldn't make it back home.

THOMAS: I never wanted to, old buddy.

BEN: That's what you tell yourself, isn't it?

THOMAS: I see what's going on.

BEN: What?

THOMAS: I finally figured it out. This is how you fucked up your marriage, isn't it? You were never home because you always had one more patient, one more wellness seminar to go to, and when it's all gone to shit you write to Jess for no good reason, you play Big Daddy to this kid. It's all out of order.

BEN: This has nothing to do with Jess.

THOMAS: Doesn't it? You think that by going out on a limb for this total stranger somehow what happened with you and Jess and the baby can be erased.

BEN: Man, you've got balls. We lost a child.

THOMAS: I know you did. And I'm sorry, I told you that, but—

BEN: You have no idea what it means—

THOMAS: I understand what you're—

BEN: Don't you dare tell me you understand!

(Beat.)

THOMAS: All I'm saying, Ben, is that this kid isn't here to help solve your problems. When you're in a place like this you have to treat people to the best of your ability, but you have to do it faster, and you can't make any attachments.

BEN: That's not the way I work, Thomas.

THOMAS: There is a line of Albanians out there just like Agim—sweet, needy, lost. Don't you think I see that?

BEN: I'm not sure you do.

THOMAS: Let me tell you something. No matter how hard you try to stay removed from these situations, somebody's story's going to get to you.

BEN: What do you know?

THOMAS: Did you hear the one about the Rwandan father who'd been on the run for months—huh? The man had walked for hundreds of miles without shoes—and how after his eight-year-old son bled to death before his very eyes because people like us weren't around, this man had to bury his boy under a banana tree with his bare fucking hands. Heard that one, Ben? I have. Want to hear another? Don't tell me I'm not listening. Thing is, despite your sympathy for this kid, we're getting maybe 12,000 more just like him tomorrow, and maybe the day after that. You can't justify rescuing one person when we—

BEN: Rescue him? I'm trying to reunite him with the only family he's got left. She's his mother, for God's sake! I mean, why are you here if you're not trying to save these Albanians from—?

THOMAS: I'm not trying to *save* anybody. I wouldn't know where to begin. But wheel them in, put them on my table, and I'll work as hard as I can as fast as I can because from where I'm standing the line isn't getting any shorter. That's why I do this, Ben. I've talked to that man; I've looked into his eyes when he talks about that banana tree. But I have to be able to function here. We can't get caught up in stories. So while you're busy with one kid, ten are out the OR doors and on their way to Skopje.

BEN: So it's all about numbers to you.

THOMAS: Look, the more people we bandage, the fewer might become statistics for some *Times* article on how history is doomed to repeat itself—again and again and again. It's why Maja's out there all night picking up as many of them as she can. We do our best. Tell me it's not enough, and I'll agree with you. But it's something. It's more than most people are willing to do. Shit, most people probably think Kosovo is some sort of fucking allergy medicine. But as sad as that is, for your own sanity (and for mine), you have to try and put any personal feelings to the back of your mind.

BEN: What if you can't?

THOMAS: Then maybe you shouldn't be here.

(THOMAS exits.)

SCENE 6

(Lights rise on YULI, eating an apple and staring at AGIM'S open hand.)

YULI: Do you see this?

AGIM: Where?

YULI: *(Pointing.)* Right there.

AGIM: I see it.

YULI: Each little notch represents a child. I count five of them.

AGIM: Five?

YULI: What's wrong with five?

AGIM: It's too many.

YULI: Says who?

AGIM: I don't want five children.

YULI: *(Holding out hand.)* Count your blessings. Look at mine: only one tiny notch.

AGIM: But you don't have any—

YULI: That's you. You're lucky you have so many.

AGIM: *(Pointing.)* What's this one?

YULI: Your lifeline. *(Tracing it.)* Look at that: it's almost to your wrist. You'll live 'til you're a hundred.

AGIM: And this?

YULI: For your heart.

AGIM: Can you read it?

YULI: It says your heart is strong. And your hands don't lie, boy. Your eyes, maybe, but never your hands. They tell you everything you need to know.

AGIM: What else do mine say?

YULI: They say—let me see—they say you've never built a house; they say you let women do your laundry; they say…

AGIM: What?

YULI: They say you're young.

(YULI strokes AGIM'S hand. Beat.)

YULI (Cont'd): So, how did you like her, huh? Not so bad. Do not tell me she was your first. *(AGIM pulls his hand away.)* My advice? Get what you can now. *(Beat.)* Ah! Good bread, warm pussy, and a little money in our pockets to boot. Not a bad day all in all. If you had not convinced me to let her go we could have kept her for awhile, brought her along with us— good for a few days, you know? I think she would have liked it. But no! Mr. Sentimental. *(Mocking AGIM)* "We have to let her go, Yuli. We have to let her go." Oh well, I am being hard on you, aren't I? You are good boy, but you need direction. Not all that unusual at your age. What are you now? Seventeen? Eighteen?

AGIM: Almost twenty.

YULI: Twenty? You have got a young face. That is what it is—a young face. Anybody ever tell you that?

AGIM: You have.

YULI: I have. Sure. Be thankful, because when you start getting the creases—jowls too—you might as well kiss sweet youth goodbye. People used to tell me I had young face, but look at me now.

AGIM: I do not care how I look.

YULI: That is what we all say at twenty. You are just lucky I am around.

AGIM: Why?

YULI: All boys need someone. A mother may be the most important—I will grant you that—but you cannot just replace a father, now can you?

AGIM: You are not my father.

YULI: A father is more than blood, you know.

AGIM: You are not my father.

YULI: I should have been!

AGIM: But you are not. You never will be.

YULI: Plenty of people your age never had their father for one stinking day. But here I sit trying to teach you thing or two. And what have I got to show for it? Back talk. Contempt. Sooner or later you will see what I have done for you. And you will thank me for it. *(Notices AGIM'S journal.)* What is that there?

AGIM: Nothing.

YULI: Stop fucking with me, boy. What is it? Where did it come from?

AGIM: It's a notebook—just a notebook.

YULI: For what?

AGIM: To write things down in.

YULI: You are a writer now. Yesterday a schoolteacher, last week a fireman.

AGIM: I never wanted to be a fireman.

YULI: When you were seven you did. I remember. *(Beat.)* Anything special you write?

AGIM: Thoughts. Letters.

YULI: Letters? To who? To who?!

AGIM: Mother.

YULI: *(Laughing.)* What the hell is your mother going to do with a letter? The bitch cannot read.

AGIM: Do not talk about her like that.

YULI: What are you going to do about it? Huh? Well, what are you waiting for? *(AGIM backs down.)* I thought so.

(AGIM sits. Pause.)

AGIM: I thought maybe if I told her...I was...thinking...

YULI: Thinking, thinking, always thinking. Just like me.

AGIM: I am not like you at all.

YULI: You can say that now, but you will see. You would be lost without me, boy. Do not ever forget that. *(Beat.)* You going to eat that radish?

(BEN enters. Lights change on his first line. We can now see boxes that suggest this is a storage tent.)

BEN: Tired?

AGIM: No. What?

(The lights on YULI slowly fade.)

BEN: I asked whether or not you're tired.

AGIM: Has bus gone?

BEN: It's gone.

AGIM: I am cold.

(BEN opens a few boxes until he finds a blanket.)

BEN: Take this.

AGIM: Don't we need to go back to tent?

BEN: No. Stay here. I'll come and bring you food when I'm not on my rounds.

AGIM: You do this before?

BEN: Hide someone in a hospital storage tent? Oh, all the time. I'm kidding. Now, try to lay low and nobody will find you. And when your mother comes—

AGIM: *If* she comes.

BEN: *When.* She's probably crossed the border by now. She could be here in a few hours. Don't give up hope.

AGIM: It is hard. Sometimes…

BEN: What? It's okay. You can tell me.

AGIM: Sometimes I think of killing myself.

BEN: Killing yourself?

AGIM: I try once already, but the gun slip.

BEN: Your neck.

AGIM: Yes. I do that to myself.

BEN: Where's this all coming from?

AGIM: It gets bad—*inside*.

BEN: There's nothing so bad that you should ever consider—Things can change.

AGIM: Not here.

BEN: Anywhere.

AGIM: You do not know.

BEN: I do know. You just have to hold on.

AGIM: Is that what you did?

BEN: When?

AGIM: With you and your wife?

BEN: I have to get back.

(BEN tries to leave.)

AGIM: No. Please.

BEN: Look, kid, I'm doing the best I can for you, but I've got other patients—

AGIM: The day is Tuesday. Family gets word from neighbors that police have told all Albanians to go from whole town. The family is surprised because these neighbors—Serbs—tell them in way to make it seem real—very real. These Serb neighbors have lived next door for twelve years, but today they speak in ugly tones. But Albanian family stays. What can police do? They broke no laws, committed no crimes. TV is on and two small children—girls—, their teen-age brother, and mother are happy. What have they to worry about? And when threatened time comes and nothing happens, family—they have paid no attention to time—think it is all okay. Turn the channel. But police do come. One of twins hears them first. Girl goes into kitchen for glass of water. It is hot today. The little girl sees one of policeman break kitchen window. These police wear masks—not like police at all— The police carry no rifles or grenades—why would a policeman carry such thing? They barge in through back door while family sits on couch watching Bugs Bunny. They surprise one of twins, who drops her tall glass of water. Mother hears breaking glass and senses danger. She remembers threats of her neighbors and tells her teenage son to hide in basement. They will never hurt little girls, but young men must be hidden.

So man of house—only sixteen—stumbles down basement stairs to hide just as police come into living room. There are ten of them. Without a word little girls are shot in head. Mother screams; she is punched in stomach. She goes down and crawls toward her murdered daughters. And now a man—your age, older—grabs her hair to get a grip before he takes out his cock. She screams when he gets on top of her, children's bodies nearby. Then, other men perform tricks silently…One after another finishes with her and goes toward street.

Then the last one—young, no beard—cries, doesn't want to. Boy is laughed at by first man, but others have gone and even first man forgets about young one's tears and he is ordered to check basement for more. He moves to top of stairs. And then slowly, like sleepwalker—A creak is heard in darkness, but where? Basement is small. It won't take long to find boy. I…I hear his breathing—like someone drowning far away—gurgle—catching breath. Then white. Eyes? I aim at white—I squeeze trigger three times quick. Bang! Bang! Bang!

BEN: What are you… talking about?

AGIM: Nothing. Nothing…It is calm now. Dark. I feel my way to him, find him then—touch his face. Still warm. Smooth, but beard not far off.

BEN: What are you telling me?

AGIM: I have told you.

BEN: *You* killed him?

AGIM: Yes.

BEN: Who the fuck are you?!

AGIM: Maybe I am just good storyteller.

BEN: Wait—Jesus Christ! This is what you did?

AGIM: It is what happened.

BEN: And what about the mother? Huh? What about her?!

AGIM: I would not let others kill her. Yuli wanted to. She is Agim's mother. I knew her… before…

BEN: Didn't she recognize you…? I mean, how… how do you know she's still alive?

AGIM: I don't. I wrote her letter, put it into one of books I had borrowed from her. It started as to say sorry for all we had done to her, but then I wrote that her son gone and went to Brazde camp. That he escaped.

BEN: She thinks her son—the one you… you… She thinks he's… alive?

AGIM: If your whole family was murdered, would you not believe—want badly to believe—and try and find him? If it was your child, would not you want it to be true? I need to see her again. Explain—

BEN: What's there to explain, Agim…? That's not even your real name, is it?

AGIM: I could not tell her then. Sorry that she suffered and that twins suffered and that Agim suffered. I have to look in her eyes. I have to tell her this.

BEN: There's nothing you can say to her—

AGIM: Not for her. For me. Demush.

BEN: Demush?

AGIM: Yes.

BEN: But you didn't… rape her? Tell me you didn't—

AGIM: Yuli did not pay attention. He was drunk. He thought I had, but I told you. I cried. I could not do it.

BEN: And where's your friend Yuli now, huh?

AGIM: Yuli was not my friend. He died the day after we raided house. A NATO bomb hit our truck. It is how I got hurt.

BEN: And now they want to send you away to a family of total strangers in New Jersey.

AGIM: I cannot go there. Lumina is my only chance—

BEN: At what?

AGIM: You do not understand. I thought you would understand.

BEN: Help me! Help me understand this…this fucking nightmare…

AGIM: I must see her. Please, I need you to help me—

BEN: I've done enough.

AGIM: No, listen—

BEN: The moment you lied…

AGIM: But we are friends.

BEN: How can you say that?

AGIM: A person is never one thing, Ben. I am Demush *and* Agim. The moment he died I feel him pass into me. Demush and Agim. Agim and Demush. Now, we are same thing.

(BEN goes to grab AGIM, but the boy is gone. Blackout.)

ACT II

SCENE 1

(BEN, in his cot, is reading AGIM'S journal. He looks exhausted. THOMAS'S bottle of rakija lies empty nearby. Stage left, TONYA, in silhouette, is talking on her cell phone inaudibly. After a moment, lights rise center on LUMINA sitting in a chair. A dirty bandana covers her eyes. TONYA enters.)

TONYA: Good morning.

LUMINA: Where is son?

TONYA: He's on his way. One of our doctors is bringing him over. Can I get you anything?

LUMINA: Only him.

(Lights fade on BEN.)

TONYA: *(Pouring a glass of water from a pitcher.)* It should be just a minute.

LUMINA: Too long.

TONYA: How about some water while you wait?

LUMINA: Water, yes. Please.

TONYA: *(Placing it in her hands.)* Here you go.

LUMINA: Thank you.

TONYA: Are you alright? Your hands are shaking.

LUMINA: Are they? I am… I do not know word for it in English… *(LUMINA drinks.)*

TONYA: I'm sure you're very excited. Would you like some more?

LUMINA: Yes.

(TONYA pours more.)

LUMINA (Cont'd): I am very thirsty.

TONYA: You've had a long trip.

(THOMAS enters.)

THOMAS: *(To TONYA.)* I need to talk to you.

TONYA: Oh, Thomas, I want to introduce you to Agim's mother. Mrs. Arifi, this is one of our doctors, Thomas Mandelbaum.

THOMAS: Good to meet you.

LUMINA: You take care of boy?

THOMAS: Yeah, we did. Nice kid. *(Turning to TONYA.)* Tonya, I'm on the recovery schedule for Tuesday night, right?

TONYA: You're on it. You'll just have to gas up the truck.

THOMAS: Sure.

(AGIM enters. He slowly approaches LUMINA and drops to his knees before her. He takes her hand and kisses it. THOMAS and TONYA watch for a moment.)

LUMINA: Is you, boy? *(No response.)* Is you?

AGIM: It is me.

LUMINA: Speak up. I cannot hear you.

AGIM: It is me, yes. What happened to your eyes?

LUMINA: Explosion near truck, that is all. Lights very bright. It is sure to pass. Come, let me touch you, boy. People don't like to touch out there on roads, in trucks. I must touch you.

(THOMAS and TONYA turn away from them and continue talking together, inaudibly, until they fade into darkness.)

AGIM: You must be tired.

LUMINA: Come and let me see.

(AGIM sits up directly in front of WOMAN, facing audience. WOMAN opens her arms and embraces him. While in the embrace, she breathes him in deeply.)

LUMINA: What are you wearing? Is it perfume? Since when…? Since when do you smell like a… like a… *(She touches his face.)* Agim? *(Pause. She removes bandage from her eyes, which are closed and black.)* Come. Let me wipe off smell. *(She dabs AGIM'S face with her bandage.)* It has been so long. I missed doing things for you. *(She slowly passes the scarf around his neck.)* Like a mother should for her son. Like a mother should!

71

BEN'S VOICE: No…

(LUMINA pulls scarf taut, opens her eyes wide, and slowly strangles AGIM, his eyes bulging out of his head.)

BEN: Noooooo!

(BEN awakes from his nightmare.)

SCENE 2

(Night. Hospital noises. THOMAS, in his surgical scrubs, is preparing for the OR. He has a clipboard in his hands.)

TONYA: *(From offstage.)* Thomas? Thomas?

THOMAS: Out here.

TONYA: Where?

THOMAS: Here!

TONYA: *(Entering.)* Oh. We need to talk.

THOMAS: Make it quick, huh? They're prepping another amputation. Fourth one today—go figure.

TONYA: I won't keep you long, but I thought you should know about this before the whole camp...

THOMAS: I'm flattered, Tonya, but although I find you very attractive—

TONYA: Will you shut up a minute? Just shut up. I got a call twenty minutes ago. Shit.

THOMAS: What's going on, Ritter?

TONYA: The recovery team was found murdered this morning about a mile from here—near the border. Hurley, Reese, and... and Maja Radulovic. *(Pause.)* I'm sorry. *(Pause.)* Are you alright? *(Silence.)* Thomas.

THOMAS: I'm okay.

TONYA: Are you sure?

THOMAS: I'm fine.

TONYA: I don't believe you.

THOMAS: Believe whatever you want.

TONYA: Look, I know this is—

THOMAS: Tonya, would you just shut the fuck up!

(Long silence. TONYA moves to exit.)

THOMAS: What made you come back?

TONYA: What?

THOMAS: Why'd you come back here?

TONYA: What do you mean?

THOMAS: The day we got here you said you left. After Haiti, you stopped. Every year I buy myself a one way ticket home, but for some reason I never make it to the airport.

TONYA: When I was in Haiti, my mother sent me word that she was ill. So I went home. She held on for a few years, but… My friends don't understand why I do this. Whenever I go home, the people I love the most tell me what a waste my whole life has been. They don't understand that I need to… So I come back.

(THOMAS gently reaches out, almost touches her.)

TONYA: Look, if there's anything—

THOMAS: No.

TONYA: Because—

THOMAS: Tonya.

TONYA: Yes.

THOMAS: There's nothing.

TONYA: You're sure—

THOMAS: Really.

TONYA: Then I, um, I better…

THOMAS: You better, yeah. You better…

(TONYA pauses, looks at him, and then exits. Pause. THOMAS looks down at his hands and sees that they are shaking. After a moment, he moves to exit. Lights fade.)

SCENE 3

(Night. AGIM is disoriented, confused. He clutches the Bulls hat. YULI, near him, lies broken and bleeding.)

AGIM: Where is the pain?

YULI: I do not know.

AGIM: There is a lot of blood.

YULI: It looks worse than it is.

AGIM: We need to find a doctor.

YULI: I am tough, boy. You should know this by now.

AGIM: But there has to be someone here who can—

YULI: All Albanians, and I do not want their help.

AGIM: What does it matter who helps? If they can fix you—

YULI: You still do not see, do you?

AGIM: All I see is—

YULI: I told you—

AGIM: You are going to die if we—

YULI: No! Leave it. Just stay with me a little while. I only need to rest for a time.

AGIM: I could find you water. You must be thirsty.

YULI: Why do you care what happens to me, huh? I would think you would be happy to see me like this.

AGIM: No...

YULI: I know what you think of me, boy. You do not hide it. I see in your eyes—

AGIM: But you are suffering.

YULI: There is worse pain than this.

AGIM: I know.

YULI: Do you?

AGIM: Yes.

YULI: You try so hard.

AGIM: To do what?

YULI: To fight it—to stop being what you are. But soon, you will realize that the more you try to escape what you are, the more you become it.

AGIM: You are weak—

YULI: Not so.

AGIM: Very weak.

YULI: You will remember my words. *(Beat.)* Here. *(Referring to his gun.)* Take this; you will need it. Go on. What are you waiting for, boy?

(AGIM moves to him, takes the gun, and holds it in his hand.)

YULI (Cont'd): How does it feel? *(Silence.)* You'll get used to it. *(Pause. Looking at his own hand.)* Let me see. I wonder what it says now. Take a look.

(AGIM holds YULI'S hand and looks into it.)

AGIM: I can't read it.

YULI: Look closer.

AGIM: I don't know how.

(Silence.)

YULI: Maybe you are best to leave me.

AGIM: I am staying with you. You take care of me and now...

YULI: Now it is your turn.

AGIM: Yes.

YULI: Remember when you had the chicken pox and I made you tea—

AGIM: And we sang songs by the fire.

YULI: You like when I take care of you like that.

AGIM: That was a good day.

(YULI moans in pain.)

AGIM (Cont'd): What is wrong?

YULI: I am a little cold. That is all.

(AGIM takes off his jacket and puts it around YULI.)

YULI (Cont'd): Will you do something for me? Will you sing to me? I've always loved to hear you sing... You have a good voice.

AGIM: Really?

YULI: You do.

AGIM: What should I sing?

YULI: It doesn't matter.

(Pause.)

AGIM: I cannot think of anything.

YULI: Please...

*(AGIM hums softly **You Are My Sunshine**.)*

YULI (Cont'd): I like that one. Where did you learn it?

AGIM: My mother.

YULI: Keep singing. *(Beat.)* Look at all that blood, will you? It looks so different when it is your own—so red. Do you see it, boy? It is everywhere—on your clothes too—on your shirt and...and your shoes. It will never come clean now.

AGIM: "…Please don't take my sunshine away."

YULI: Never…

(YULI is dead. AGIM rises, takes the gun, and exits.)

SCENE 4

(THOMAS is lounging on his bed; BEN enters and sits on his. Silence.)

THOMAS: Remember the first time we saw my father in surgery? What were we—ten or eleven? It was like going to the movies or something—the color of the light; the quiet; the stillness. And my father standing at the center like a god. We both knew, didn't we? From that moment, we knew we wanted to be doctors. Everything THOMAS (cont'd): was so clear...and simple... *(Pause.)* So how the fuck did we get here, Ben? Huh? What happened? *(Pause. Gazing at chessboard.)* Good players have this ability to see five, six moves ahead at all times. And if you play enough you can train yourself to avoid the traps. You use your imagination and play out in your mind all the possible moves your opponent might make. I mean, there could be hundreds. But if you practice, focus your mind, you can beat just about anybody, right? Then one day, Kasparov walks in and you know you're fucked. You can bluff, sure, but he'll see you sweating. You're thinking five moves ahead, but he's thinking seven. You know what you do then? Huh? I'll tell you what you do: you politely stand up, shake the man's hand, and throw your chessboard in the trash.

(Silence.)

BEN: Thomas, I'm sorry.

THOMAS: I pretended that it couldn't really reach us— like there was a force field around this place—but it did.

BEN: Yeah, it did.

THOMAS: This kind of shit doesn't happen to us.

BEN: It's not supposed to.

THOMAS: But who are we kidding, huh? You keep your head down, do your work, and at the end of the day you still get shot at. So what am I supposed to do now?

BEN: I don't know.

THOMAS: I tried to keep moving, you know, just kept pushing the rock up the hill. But sometimes you've got to wonder if you're...

BEN: You're a good doctor, Thomas.

THOMAS: Maybe, but I sure as hell ain't God.

BEN: Took you this long to figure that out?

THOMAS: Guess I'm kind of slow.

BEN: I could've told you that.

THOMAS: So why didn't you? It would've saved me a shit load of time.

(BEN removes the bottle of rakija from beneath his cot and opens it. He offers it to THOMAS but is waved off.)

THOMAS (Cont'd): I'm fucking beat.

(THOMAS rolls over, away from BEN; BEN swigs from the bottle in silence.)

BEN: Jess left me. Did I ever tell you that? I came home late one night—shit, I was always coming home late—and the house was empty: bed was unmade; her clothes were everywhere. She was just...gone. And you know, like a fucking idiot I wrote her a letter every week for six months, but nothing. Not one word. Until yesterday.

THOMAS: Yesterday?

(BEN pulls out a letter and tosses it on the chessboard.)

THOMAS (Cont'd): Why didn't you say anything?

BEN: Since when do I have to tell you everything? Anyway, I had other things on my mind.

THOMAS: What could be more important than—? Wait, you didn't even open it?

BEN: Snowed like hell the day he was born. And from the start I knew something was wrong. You know how babies are born with those small holes in their hearts, and how they usually close up right after birth? Well, his never did. There was nothing they could do. It's funny how you go through all those years of school, all those years of medical training, only to find that when you need it most it's all so useless. Afterwards, they brought him to me—I wanted to see him. At first, I didn't think I did but when the time came I told them to bring him out. They'd dressed him up in little blue pants and sweater, a knit hat to keep his head warm. He looked like a doll, but he wasn't. He was a real baby, so small. His eyes were closed as if he was sleeping. And I remember thinking, this is my son. I'm holding my son. But I couldn't cry. I don't know why.

I just couldn't cry. *(Beat.)* How are you supposed to go on after something like that, you know? But you do. Jess and I were like two ghosts living in that house. I think maybe I was looking for her to say something to make it all go away, but she never said a word. And then one day—it seemed like months later—I woke up and he wasn't the first thing I thought about. He was the second thing, but he wasn't the first. That was the day she left. *(Beat.)* So, go ahead. Open it.

THOMAS: She sent it to you.

BEN: It's kind of funny, isn't it—how you called me that night? You'd just gotten in from the airport, remember? I met you at your hotel. And before you'd even bought me a beer I knew I was coming with you this time. It was so unlike me. But I thought, Why the hell not? I've got nothing left to lose. Then I got here, and it was total shit.

THOMAS: Yeah.

BEN: I mean, what was I doing? I was in way over my head right from the start, and I knew it. But then one day that kid walked through the door and everything else disappeared. I was going to help him, no matter what it took; I was going to give him the help I could never give my own... *(Pause.)* It was like I saw things clearly for the first time in a long time; for a second I figured I had control over something in my fucked up little life.

THOMAS: But you let him go, Ben. That's what all this means. In the end, you finally let him go.

BEN: Did I?

THOMAS: Sure you did, and that's what's important, right? It's over. Come on, now, open the letter.

(THOMAS holds out the letter to him; BEN doesn't take it.)

BEN: You up for a game? *(He begins setting up the chess board.)* What do you say we make this interesting? Let's see, I've got twenty bucks right here says I can take you.

THOMAS: You've got to be shitting me.

BEN: Come on, come on, I'm growing a beard here.

THOMAS: You're getting a second chance, Ben. This is what you've been waiting for.

BEN: Two weeks ago you thought I was crazy to write her.

THOMAS: I didn't think you were—

BEN: Yeah, you did. And you were right.

THOMAS: Really, Ben, this just isn't like you.

BEN: A person is never one thing, Thomas. *(He swigs his drink and moves his pawn.)* You gonna move?

(THOMAS stares at BEN as lights fade.)

SCENE 5

(Light rises on TONYA talking on the phone and pulling a cigarette pack from her shirt pocket. The pack is empty. Frustrated, she crushes it and begins digging in a drawer for another.)

TONYA: *(Into phone.)* He was supposed to be on rounds...And you have no idea—Uh huh, I'm just worried... I hope so too... Now, is the shift being covered, or are patients simply—*(She finds a fresh pack of cigarettes.)* And what about Agim? Any sign of him? He wasn't on the bus... Well, keep looking. He couldn't have gone too far... Uh huh...

(As she opens the cigarettes, a well-maintained woman—LUMINA—enters carrying a suitcase. LUMINA is quite unlike the woman in BEN's dream.)

LUMINA: Where do I go?

TONYA: Could you wait outside?

LUMINA: I have been waiting long enough.

TONYA: New patients—

LUMINA: I am not a patient; I am looking for my—

TONYA: *(Into phone.)* Hold on, Denise. *(To LUMINA.)* If you're not a patient, then you'll have to fill out a registration form in tent 23. Buses to the holding camp run every three hours. If you go out here, past the big green supply tent—

LUMINA: I—

TONYA: *Thank you!*

LUMINA: I am here for my son Agim.

TONYA: Agim?

LUMINA: I am Lumina Arifi.

TONYA: *(Into phone.)* Denise, get Reid to cover the shift. And if you see Ben, send him over here, pronto. *(Hangs up. To LUMINA.)* Mrs. Arifi, I didn't realize who you—

LUMINA: Do you speak to all of the refugees this way?

TONYA: Things are a bit difficult at the moment. I apologize.

LUMINA: He is not hurt is he?

TONYA: Agim's fine. Now, why don't you sit down for a moment?

LUMINA: I'll stand. Thank you.

TONYA: When did you arrive?

LUMINA: A truck brought me in twenty minutes ago. Who are you?

TONYA: I'm Tonya Ritter. I coordinate the hospital here.

LUMINA: You are in charge.

TONYA: That's right.

LUMINA: Then why is all this taking so long? I have already seen three different people, and no one seems to know to whom I should speak.

TONYA: You've come to the right place.

LUMINA: But where is my son?

TONYA: We're... we're trying to locate him.

LUMINA: You mean he is missing?

TONYA: Temporarily. We have a large facility here, as you saw.

LUMINA: How could this happen? How could you have just—?

TONYA: This is a camp, not a prison, Mrs. Arifi. He's being looked for. Now, the best thing to do is stay in one place.

LUMINA: But where could he be?

TONYA: Agim's become good friends with one of our doctors. When we find the doctor, we may find Agim. The two of them spend a lot of time together. Seems they share a love of literature.

LUMINA: Literature?

TONYA: Literature: reading, words.

LUMINA: I speak English well enough, Ms. Ritter. We had many books back home. I am a college professor. Physics. But I don't recall Agim reading many books.

TONYA: Well, he's been a voracious reader while he's been here.

LUMINA: You must be mistaken. Agim never read my…

TONYA: Are you alright? Mrs. Arifi?

LUMINA: I'm fine.

TONYA: Would you like some water?

LUMINA: *(Referring to TONYA's cigarettes.)* I'll take one of those.

TONYA: *(Offering.)* Please.

(LUMINA takes a cigarette from the pack.)

LUMINA: Thank you. I'm surprised you smoke.

TONYA: *(Lighting both of their cigarettes.)* I don't. Well, I do, once in a while. Great stress reliever.

LUMINA: For me as well.

TONYA: And today's been—*Every day*'s been…

LUMINA: You have enormous responsibility.

TONYA: Yes, but we manage. The refugees have it worse. There's no comparison.

LUMINA: No, there's not.

(Pause.)

TONYA: So when was the last time you saw Agim?

LUMINA: One month ago—almost. The police had come for us. I sent Agim to hide in the basement. I knew the Serbs would be looking for the men. When they came... They spared my life; I don't know why. *(Pause.)* You treated my boy?

TONYA: Yes, we did.

LUMINA: What was wrong?

TONYA: He had a superficial wound from a gunshot and some minor—

LUMINA: Agim was shot?

TONYA: Yes, but he's okay now. It's healed quite nicely. I've seen much worse.

LUMINA: You saved his life then. *(Beat.)* Tell me, have there been many reunions?

TONYA: Some. Not as many as you might think. We have *some* resources to do searches for patients' loved ones. We do our best, but even that could never be enough.

LUMINA: You underestimate us.

TONYA: I'm not sure what you mean?

LUMINA: You did not think I would come, did you?

TONYA: I hoped—

LUMINA: Did you?

TONYA: No. I knew the chances—

LUMINA: Were small.

TONYA: Yes.

LUMINA: But I did come.

TONYA: Yes, you did.

LUMINA: Why did you?

TONYA: Why?

LUMINA: There must be a reason.

TONYA: I'm not sure what you want me to say.

LUMINA: We are not real to most of you, are we? Even
now, you sit across from me, but you do not see *me*,
do you? Not really. You work here for months at a
time; you imagine you know who we are because you
read descriptions in a guidebook; and then you arrive
to fix it all somehow. But the facts of my life remain.
What they did to me... I cannot tell others—other Albanians. I could never go back. It is worse than death,
you see, where I come from.

TONYA: I'm sorry.

LUMINA: I do not tell you because I want you to feel
sorry for me. I simply tell you so you will know.
These facts cannot be changed, no matter what I do. It
is futile you see. There is always an again and again
and again, no matter what *you* do. In the end, the victims are destined to become the murderers, and there
is nothing you can do about it.

(AGIM enters from the shadows; they turn to him.)

TONYA: Agim, where have you been? We've been looking for you.

(Silence.)

LUMINA: Are we finished, Ms. Ritter?

TONYA: Yes, of course. I'll have to get the papers for
you to sign. It won't take long. I'm glad everything
worked out the way it was supposed to.

LUMINA: Yes.

TONYA: I just wish Dr. Gold was here. He's the doctor I
was telling you about. Agim, I'm sure you'd like to
say goodbye.

LUMINA: Please thank him for us.

TONYA: I will. He'll be glad to hear your story had a
happy ending. The bus leaves in a little while; you'll
both be in New Jersey in a couple of days.

LUMINA: My brother hasn't seen Agim since he was a
boy. He'll hardly recognize him.

(TONYA'S cell phone rings.)

TONYA: I'll be back in ten minutes with those papers.
(She answers her phone and moves to exit.) Ritter...
Oh, thank God. Uh huh, right... well, I don't care
what his excuse is. Tell him to get his ass over to tent
12 ASAP...Ben and I are going to have ourselves a
nice little chat...

(She's gone. Silence.)

LUMINA: What have you done with him? What have you done with my son? All I want is my son. I want to touch his face. I do not care about myself. The girls are dead. They are in the hands of Allah.

AGIM: Agim is dead.

LUMINA: Dead...? Dead...? Dead.

AGIM: Killed that day...

LUMINA: By who? You and that band of marauders—the ones you came with?

AGIM: It all happened so fast...

(The sounds of screaming and gunfire. Lights rise on YULI, orchestrating the chaos.)

LUMINA: The girls dead, Yuli and his men finished with me, and you... waiting. You were one of them.

AGIM: No...

LUMINA: In that moment, I hated you like I hated them. I heard him call to you...

YULI: You—Demush—your turn, boy!

(YULI pushes AGIM toward LUMINA.)

LUMINA: He wanted me to know, even with your masks on. He wanted me to know that it was you and he who were doing these things to us.

AGIM: No, not me... not me...

LUMINA: You were a frightened rabbit, eyes darting—

AGIM: There was blood running down between your legs; Yuli kept shouting at me.

YULI: What's the rush, boy? Take your time.

AGIM: I could not do it.

YULI: *(Distracted. To unseen others.)* Hey, I like those plates. Stick them in the bag. This cunt always had nice things. Yeah those! Don't break any.

AGIM: I wanted to die.

LUMINA: But you did not. Agim did.

YULI: *(To AGIM.)* Come here! The boy is in the basement. Take the gun.

(YULI hands AGIM a pistol. AGIM walks toward basement, freezes in tableau. Silence.)

LUMINA: What happened?

(AGIM turns and approaches YULI.)

YULI: Did you do it?

LUMINA: Tell me what happened!

YULI: Did you shoot the little fucker?

LUMINA: What did he say? I could not hear?

(AGIM pulls the Chicago Bulls hat from his back pocket and gives it to YULI.)

YULI: Ha ha! Good boy. Good.

LUMINA: What did he *say*?

(YULI puts the hat on AGIM'S head.)

YULI: Take it as a keepsake—your first time.

LUMINA: What did *you* say?

AGIM: I said it is done.

(LUMINA spits in AGIM'S face. Lights on YULI fade.)

LUMINA: You're just like the rest of them.

AGIM: No—

LUMINA: A pig like all the others—

AGIM: No!

LUMINA: What are you then? I'll tell you what you are:
You're a filthy coward, a liar—!

AGIM: Shhh! Ritter will hear you.

LUMINA: And when she comes back I'm going to tell
her all about you. Why shouldn't I? Stop looking at
me!

AGIM: Here. *(He pulls YULI'S gun from his pocket and
presents it to her.)* It was Yuli's.

LUMINA: That?

AGIM: Take it.

LUMINA: What am I supposed to do?

AGIM: Shoot me.

LUMINA: Is it so easy then?

AGIM: It should be. I killed your son. I watched him die.

(LUMINA suddenly grabs the gun and points it at him.)

LUMINA: Where do I stick it, huh? What about your head, so I can fire and watch your brains paint the ceiling? Or, your heart instead—just pull the trigger and reach my hand into your chest and pull out what's left. Maybe I should just watch you bleed to death. Which way should it be?

AGIM: I don't know...

LUMINA: Is that all you can say? Get on your knees. Get on your knees! *(He does. She places the gun barrel between his eyes.)* This is why you came here, isn't it? This is why you told these doctors you were my son. Answer me!

AGIM: Yes.

LUMINA: Louder!

AGIM: Yes!

LUMINA: It's what you've wanted all this time—for me to find you and do this, put you out of your misery.

AGIM: You have to. You are a victim; I am a murderer. If you want to help me, do it. Do it, please! Do it!

LUMINA: But I don't want to help you, can't you see that? I want to choke you until your skin turns blue and you gasp for air, but I don't want to help you. You want death, but I won't be the one to give it to you. You deserve so much worse than that.

(She lowers the gun.)

AGIM: Please, I beg you, you must—

LUMINA: Why, so you can meet your fate bravely like Agim did—redeem yourself somehow? That's too easy. You are not Agim; you are Demush, and you are not brave, so don't pretend otherwise. Now, get off your knees, you pathetic, sniveling little boy.

(Long silence.)

AGIM: What happens now?

LUMINA: We find our way out.

AGIM: I can't go with you.

LUMINA: You have no choice.

AGIM: Your family will kill me when they find out—

(She raises the gun and again points it at him, getting very close.)

LUMINA: Isn't that what you want—to die? Huh? Then it will all be over, won't it? Perhaps I should just turn the gun on myself then. What have I to live for, after all? You've taken away all I had. *(Pause. Again, she lowers the gun.)* Don't worry, I won't let my brother harm you; I won't tell them what you did. For all they'll know, I saved you from a life of crime and murder.

AGIM: But why?

LUMINA: Because I want to keep you close. You were the last to see my son alive, and when I look into your eyes, I'll see what he saw. When I smell your breath, I'll smell what he smelled. So, like the enemy you are, I'll keep you closer, closer than you can bear—until my pain breaks you into a million pieces.

(AGIM suddenly grabs her hand with the gun, puts the barrel to his heart and pulls the trigger. He slumps to the ground dead. Pause. LUMINA, gun still in her hand, stands stunned. BEN enters and sees LUMINA hovering above the body. She looks up, sees him, and drops the gun.)

BEN: What did you do? What did you do to him?

LUMINA: He grabbed my hand; he shot himself.

(BEN checks the boy's wound.)

BEN: Oh, Jesus.

LUMINA: It's no use.

BEN: But he can't die like this! I'm supposed to save him. I'm supposed to know what to do to save his life.

LUMINA: There's nothing you can do.

BEN: I tried to help him.

LUMINA: He didn't want your help. He wanted to die.

BEN: It didn't have to be this way.

LUMINA: What did he tell you?

BEN: He told me he wasn't your son.

LUMINA: My son is dead.

BEN: So is mine.

LUMINA: Sometimes we are helpless...

(BEN looks down at the boy, bends low to him, touching his face, his hat. He cradles the boy in his arms and begins to weep as lights very slowly fade to black.)

END OF PLAY

NOTES

www.ingramcontent.com/pod-product-compliance
Lightning Source LLC
Chambersburg PA
CBHW062009040426
42447CB00010B/1983